# HABITATS

## eXTREME FACTS

## BY STEFFI CAVELL-CLARKE

# BookLife
## PUBLISHING

©BookLife Publishing Ltd. 2019

ISBN: 978-1-786378-17-0

**Distributed by:**
Independent Publishers Group
814 N. Franklin Street
Chicago, IL 60610

**Written by:**
Steffi Cavell-Clarke

**Edited by:**
Holly Duhig

**Designed by:**
Danielle Rippengill

# CONTENTS

Words that look like this can be found in the glossary on page 24.

# HABITATS

A habitat is a place where an animal lives. It can provide an animal with food, water and shelter. There are many different sorts of habitat around the world.

Rainforests

Grasslands

Oceans

Deserts

Different types of habitat are home to different types **of animal.**

Animals often <u>adapt</u> to suit their habitats. We'll take a closer look at this later!

Animals can also help the habitats that they live in.

This in turn can help other animals living there too.

Some animals eat the plants and <u>recycle</u> the <u>nutrients</u> back into the soil, which helps other plants to grow.

Birds help to spread seeds by eating fruit and passing the seeds out in their droppings.

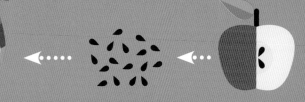

Together, animals and their habitats help to keep the <u>environment</u> healthy.

# OCEANS

An ocean habitat is a very large area of salty sea water.

Oceans cover around 71% of the Earth's surface.

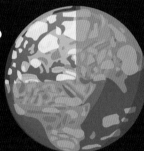

That's a big home for lots of different animals and plants.

There are rocks, sand, mud and seaweed on the ocean floor, **where many animals make their homes.**

Some animals that live in the ocean eat the plants that grow there.

Some eat other animals, such as fish, that live there too.

**Fish have adapted to their water environments in many amazing ways.**

**All fish have gills**

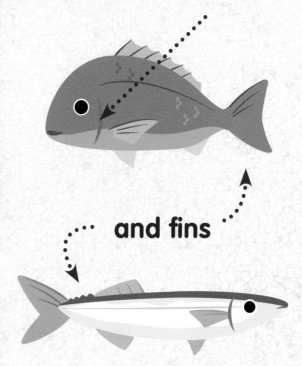

**and fins**

**Some fish can change their colors to help them blend in to their habitats. This is called camouflage.**

**which allow them to breathe and swim underwater.**

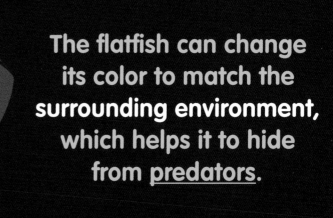

**The flatfish can change its color to match the surrounding environment, which helps it to hide from predators.**

# CORAL REEFS

You may think that coral reefs are made up of rocks, but coral reefs are actually made up of living organisms called polyps.

When polyps die, they become hard and new polyps grow on top of them.

Coral reefs are found in warm, <u>coastal</u> waters in <u>tropical</u> areas of the world.

The Great Barrier Reef is the biggest coral reef on Earth. It is 1,200 miles long. It's so big that you can see it from space!

Coral reefs are excellent habitats for fish because they provide plenty of food and shelter.

Thousands of other sea creatures live in coral reefs, such as fish, turtles, sharks and sting rays.

**Fish that live in coral reefs** are often very brightly colored so they are **camouflaged** against colorful corals.

Clownfish live inside a type of <u>venomous</u> polyp called a sea anemone. Sea anemones help to protect clownfish from predators.

Clownfish have adapted over a very long time so the anemone's venom does not affect them, but it can harm other animals including their predators.

# ISLANDS

Islands are areas of land that are completely surrounded by water.

Some islands are very large and many different types of habitats and animals can be found on them.

Some islands can be very small, but many <u>species</u> of animal can still live on them.

**Madagascar** is a large island off the south-east coast of Africa.

It is home to thousands of animals that can't be found anywhere else on the planet.

The **panther chameleon** is among the largest chameleons in the world and can be found in **Madagascar.**

A panther chameleon can grow to be the size of a cat!

Their skin colors can be red, blue, dark green or blue-green with different patterns of stripes and spots.

# GRASSLANDS

Grasslands are large, open areas of land that are covered in different grasses.

The biggest grasslands can be found in **South America**.

In the **wet** season, grasslands have very heavy rain.

But in the **dry** season there is **very little rainfall**.

Due to the **lack of rainfall** in the dry season, different species often gather around the same <u>watering hole</u> for a much-needed **drink**.

The grasslands in Africa are home to many species of animal, such as lions, zebras, elephants and wildebeest.

Smaller animals, such as snakes, mice and rabbits, can also live in the grasslands and they will often use the grass to hide from predators.

Birds use the wide, open grasslands to search for their <u>prey</u> while flying high in sky.

# DESERTS

A desert is an area that receives very little rainfall all year round.

Many deserts are hot places but some are cold.

The coldest continent, Antarctica, is actually the largest desert on Earth!

The Sahara desert in Africa is the largest hot desert in the world. The temperature can reach over 116°F!

Not many plants or animals can live in hot deserts, but those that do live there have adapted to help them to survive with very little water.

The cactus is a type of plant that can be found it hot deserts. A cactus plant stores water in its stem.

A cactus has lots of <u>roots</u>, which help it collect as much water as possible when it rains.

Camels have humps that store fat, which can be used as both food and water sources for the animal.

Ever heard of a blind skink? **They are legless, blind reptiles.**

Over thousands of years, they have adapted to living in the desert by slithering under the sand in the daytime to protect themselves against the Sun's hot rays.

# RAINFORESTS

Rainforests are forests with many trees. They are mostly found in tropical areas, around the Earth's equator. They usually experience heavy rainfall.

The **Amazon** rainforest is the **largest** tropical rainforest in the world.

From the treetops to the forest floor, every part of the rainforest is teeming with animal life.

There are more species of animal living in the tropical rainforests than anywhere else on Earth.

Rainforests are full of tall trees and thick plants, which provide both food and shelter for the many animals that live there.

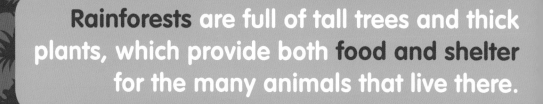

Many animals **that live in rainforests** can only survive in this habitat.

Scientists are discovering different species of insect every single day in tropical rainforests.

Leafcutter ants cut leaves off plants and carry them back to their underground nests.

Each ant can carry up to **20 times** its own body weight!

Orangutans make their homes in the trees. They are the largest tree-living animals in the world.

# POLAR REGIONS

Planet Earth has two polar regions, which are the most northern and the most southern parts of the world.

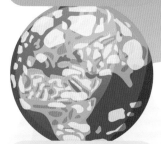

**North Pole**

They are the **coldest parts** of the planet and they are covered in **snow and ice**.

The ice can be up to **13** feet thick.

**South Pole**

The temperature can fall **below -40°F in the South Pole.**

The polar regions are the harshest environments in the world, but some animals and plants have adapted to survive in these conditions.

Polar bears live in the **North Pole** and other northern parts of the world.

When they are tired, they **dig shallow pits in the snow** to sleep in.

They also have big, **flat feet** that are good for walking on **soft snow.**

**The South Pole is home to the emperor penguin.**

They **huddle together** to keep warm in the coldest of weathers.

They are the **biggest** species of penguin in the world.

# MOUNTAINS

Mountains are large areas of land made from rock that rise above the Earth's surface.

The **highest mountain** on Earth is Mount Everest, which is **over 29,000 feet high!**

Mountain habitats can be extremely hard to survive in. They often have little food, very cold temperatures and steep, rocky slopes.

The highest part of a mountain is called its peak. The peak has the coldest temperatures and is sometimes covered in snow.

The bottom part of a mountain is usually home to the most animal life as the temperature is warmer.

The Rocky Mountains in the US are home to many different habitats, such as forests and rivers.

**Grizzly bears,** mountain lions and mountain goats are **just some of the** animals that live there.

There are also many species of bird that live there. They build their homes out of <u>materials</u> that blend in with their surroundings.

**Birds build nests so that they have safe places to raise their <u>young</u>.**

# TOWNS AND CITIES

Towns and cities are <u>urban</u> habitats, which have buildings such as houses, stores and schools.

The world is home to over 7 billion humans, and they all need a place to live.

Over half of the world's population now live in towns and cities.

As towns and cities have grown in size and number, more and more natural habitats have been destroyed.

Many animals have been unable to adapt to the new, busy urban environment.

These animals have been forced to move to new habitats, or have died out because they were unable to survive.

Some species of animal have found new ways to live in towns and cities.

These animals make up the urban wildlife that live in these new, <u>man-made</u> habitats.

Rats, pigeons, foxes and racoons are all types of animal that have adapted to live in urban areas.

They often eat the trash that humans throw away and use buildings for shelter.

# GLOSSARY

| | |
|---|---|
| **adapt** | change over time to suit different conditions |
| **coastal** | near to the coast |
| **environment** | the surrounding area |
| **man-made** | not natural; made by humans |
| **materials** | things from which objects are made |
| **nutrients** | natural substances that are needed for plants to grow |
| **predators** | animals that hunt other animals for food |
| **prey** | animals that are hunted by other animals for food |
| **recycle** | used again to make something else |
| **roots** | the part of a plant that grows underground and collects water from the soil |
| **species** | a group of very similar animals or plants that are capable of producing young together |
| **tropical** | hot and humid |
| **urban** | relating to a town or city |
| **venomous** | able to produce a harmful substance that is injected through a bite or a sting |
| **watering hole** | a place where animals drink water, such as a spring |
| **young** | an animal's offspring |

# INDEX